Table of Contents

D0473839

Essential Question 2

Short Read 1
Rabbit and Coyote 4

Short Read 2
The Valiant Little Tailor 6

Word Study Read
Chi Li and the Serpent. 10

Build, Reflect, Write 11

Extended Read 1
Molly Whuppie 12

Word Study Read
Kate Shelley: A Young Hero 20

Build, Reflect, Write 21

Extended Read 2
Hercules' Quest 22

Word Study Read
Paul Bunyan and the Troublesome Mosquitoes 30

Build, Reflect, Write 31

Support for Collaborative Conversation 32

Making Meaning with Words . . . . Inside Back Cover

How do we overcome obstacles?

Remember to annotate as you read.

Notes

Rabbit and Coyote

Rabbit and Coyote are familiar characters in the trickster tales of different cultures. In some versions, clever Rabbit escapes Coyote's plans to make a meal of him. In others, Rabbit simply enjoys outwitting Coyote and making him look foolish. This adaptation shows how gullible Coyote can be when it comes to Rabbit's tricks.

1   This tale tells the story of Rabbit and Coyote. Rabbit came upon a big rock and once there, he decided to deceive, or trick, Coyote, for Rabbit knew that foolish Coyote would fall for his trick. Sure enough, soon Coyote came by and Rabbit leaned against the big rock.

2   "What are you doing, brother?" Coyote asked Rabbit.

3   Rabbit chuckled and then said in a serious voice, "Come here quickly, brother, for the sky is falling down on us. You must lean against the rock and then hold it up while I go search for a stick that will prop up the sky."

4   Coyote, of course, agreed and began holding up the rock with all his might, doing exactly what Rabbit had ordered him to do. Rabbit simply left Coyote holding the rock, and when Rabbit didn't return, Coyote shouted, "Come back, brother! The weight of the rock is making me tired." But Rabbit did not come back. He ignored Coyote's pleas.

5   Finally, Coyote gave up holding up the rock and muttered, "I'm giving up holding up this rock, even if the sky will fall on us." But when he ran away, he fell into a ravine. Rabbit never came back and poor Coyote was lost. After a while, however, he found Rabbit. And Rabbit was already planning another trick he could play on poor, foolish Coyote.

Remember to annotate as you read.

Notes

The Valiant Little Tailor

by the Brothers Grimm

Jacob and Wilhelm Grimm were brothers who lived in Germany in the late 1700s and early 1800s. They were very interested in stories and legends called folktales. The brothers collected many of these tales and put them into books that became very popular. We still read these stories today.

1   A tailor spread jam on his bread. He laid the bread near him, and continued happily sewing. In the meantime, the smell of the sweet jam attracted flies in great numbers. The little tailor drove the unbidden guests away, however the flies would not be turned away. They came back again in larger and larger numbers. The little tailor soon lost all patience. He got a bit of cloth from the hole under his worktable, and struck the flies. When he drew the cloth away and counted, there lay before him seven dead, with legs stretched out. He could not help admiring his own bravery.

2   And so the little tailor hastened to cut himself a belt and stitched it. Finally, he embroidered on it in large letters, "Seven At One Stroke."

3   The brave little tailor wanted to tell the world about his bravery. His heart wagged with joy like a lamb's tail. So he put on the belt and resolved to go forth into the world, as he thought his workshop was too small for his valor. Before he went away, he looked around the house to see if there was anything that he could take with him. He found nothing but an old cheese, which he put in his pocket. Once outside, he observed a bird that had caught itself in the thicket. It went into his pocket with the cheese.

Notes

4   Now he took to the road boldly. And as he was light and nimble, he felt no fatigue. The road led him up a mountain, and when he had reached the highest point, he met up with a powerful giant looking about him quite comfortably.

5   The little tailor went bravely up and spoke to the giant. He said, "Good day, comrade, you are sitting there overlooking the world! I am just on my way to explore the world. Would you be inclined to go on my quest with me?"

6   The giant looked contemptuously at the tailor. He said, "You ragamuffin! You miserable creature!"

7   "Oh, indeed?" answered the little tailor. He unbuttoned his coat, and showed the giant his belt. "There you may read what kind of a man I am!" The giant read, "Seven At One Stroke." He thought this meant that the tailor had won battles with seven men, so he began to feel a little respect for the tiny fellow. Nevertheless, he wished to test him first, so he took a stone in his hand and squeezed it together until water dropped out of it.

8   "Do likewise," said the giant, "if you have the strength."

9   "Is that all?" said the tailor. "That is child's play!"

10   He put his hand into his pocket and brought out the soft cheese, pressing it until the liquid ran out of it. "Faith," said the tailor, "that was a little better, wasn't it?"

11   The giant did not know what to say, as he could not believe it. Then the giant picked up a stone and threw it so high that the eye could scarcely follow it. "Now, little mite of a man, do likewise."

12   "Well thrown," said the tailor, "but, after all, the stone came down to earth again. I will throw one which shall never come back at all."

13   And he put his hand into his pocket, took out the bird, and threw it into the air. The bird, delighted with its liberty, rose, flew away, and did not come back. "How does that shot please you, comrade?" asked the tailor.

Remember to annotate as you read.

Notes

Chi Li and the Serpent

1   Many moons ago, a ferocious serpent lived in a mountain above a Chinese village. One day, to the villagers' dismay, the giant snake came down from its cave and demanded half their rice. The terrified people quickly complied. That winter, they had barely enough to eat.

2   The serpent returned the following year. The villagers pleaded with the serpent not to take their rice, but the snake just hissed disdainfully. The people handed over half their rice.

3   This went on every year for nine years until a girl named Chi Li said, "Enough! I will put an end to this!" Her parents tried to dissuade her, but Chi Li was determined.

4   The next day, she set out with a hound, a sword, and a bag of sweetened rice balls. As she neared the serpent's lair, she laid the rice balls sideways along the path. Then she and the hound hid. Drawn by the scent, the serpent soon slithered forth. It devoured one rice ball, and then another. The hound dashed out and ran wildly around the snake in a circle. The serpent tried to seize the hound, but when it went clockwise, the hound went counterclockwise, and vice versa, until the serpent was so dizzy that it toppled over.

5   Chi Li speedily jumped forward. With a mighty swing of her sword, she chopped off the serpent's head. The villagers hailed her as a hero, and everyone lived peacefully from then on.

BuildReflectWrite

Build Knowledge

Compare two events in "Rabbit and Coyote" and "The Valiant Little Tailor."
Then summarize how they are similar.

"Rabbit and Coyote"	"The Valiant Little Tailor"
Event:	Event:
Event:	Event:
Summary:	

Reflect

How do we overcome obstacles?

Based on this week's texts, write down new ideas and questions you have about the essential question.

_____

_____

_____

_____

_____

Building Research Skills

Informative/Explanatory

Imagine that you have been asked to write an informative essay about stories with characters who are talking animals or magical creatures. One of your guiding research questions is: What other stories have characters who are talking animals or magical creatures? Read and take notes from two or more sources to help you answer this question. List the sources of your information.

Remember to annotate as you read.

Notes

Molly Whuppie

an adaptation of a Scottish fairy tale

Fairy tales are a kind of folktale that have make-believe creatures and unbelievable events that don't happen in real life. Most of them start with the sentence, "Once upon a time . . ."

1   Once upon a time there was a couple who had too many children and they could not feed them, so they took the three youngest and left them in the woods. The girls wandered through the dark, frightening woods until they came upon a house. They knocked at the door and begged for food, but the woman inside said, "I can't let you in. My husband is a giant with a terrible temper. You can't be here when he comes home."

2   The girls begged harder, promising to leave before the giant came home. So the woman finally let them in and fed them, but just as they had begun to eat, a dreadful voice said:

3   "Fee, fie, fo, fum,

4   I smell the blood of some earthly ones."

5   And suddenly, before the girls could escape, the giant entered the house.

6   The giant demanded to know who was in their home, and the wife said, "It's three poor, cold, and hungry girls who will go once they eat, so leave them alone." The giant grunted, ate up a big supper, and then ordered the girls to stay. Now the giant had three daughters of his own, and the lost girls were to sleep in the same room with the giant's daughters.

7   The youngest of the three lost girls was called Molly Whuppie, and she was very clever. She noticed that before they went to bed, the giant put straw ropes around her neck and her sisters' necks, but he put gold chains around his own daughters' necks. Molly knew not to fall asleep. When she was sure all the others, especially the giant, were asleep, Molly slipped out of bed.

8   She then quickly exchanged the straw ropes on her and her sisters' necks for the gold chains that were on the giant's daughters' necks. No one woke up during the exchange and so Molly let out a deep sigh and fell asleep.

9   In the night, the giant got up. He felt for the necks with straw and picked up his daughters. As they cried out, Molly and her sisters escaped. The girls ran and ran, and never stopped on their quest for safety until they saw a grand house before them. It turned out to be a king's house so Molly went in. She told her story to the king. He said, "Well, Molly, you are a clever girl. You've managed well. But if you go back and steal the giant's sword that hangs behind his bed, I will marry your eldest sister to my eldest son." Molly said she would try.

Notes

10   So back Molly went. She managed to slip into the giant's house, and hid below the bed. The giant came home, ate up a great supper, and went to bed. Molly waited until he was sleeping soundly and snoring loudly, and then she crept out. Next, Molly reached over the giant and got down the sword, but it rattled, waking the giant. Molly ran out with the sword. The giant ran after her. They came to the "Bridge of One Hair." Molly swiftly crossed it, but the giant couldn't. The giant yelled at Molly, but Molly took the sword to the king. Her oldest sister was married to the king's oldest son.

11   The king later said, "You've managed well, Molly. But if you will steal the purse that lies under the giant's pillow, I will marry your second sister to my second son." Molly said that she would try.

12   So Molly set out for the giant's house, slipped in, and hid below the bed again. When the giant was snoring loudly and sound asleep, she crept out. She then slipped her hand under the pillow and grabbed the purse. However, as Molly was escaping, the giant woke. Molly ran and the giant ran after her. They came to the "Bridge of One Hair." Molly swiftly crossed it, but the giant couldn't. He yelled at Molly, but she took the purse to the king. Her second sister was married to the king's second son.

13   The king then said, "Molly, you are a clever girl. But if you will steal the giant's ring, I will give you my youngest son for yourself." Molly said she would try.

14   So back Molly went to the giant's house, and hid herself under the bed. The giant ate a huge meal and then went to his bed. Shortly he was snoring loudly. Molly crept out and took hold of the giant's hand. Swiftly she pulled the ring off the giant's finger. But before she could run, the giant gripped her by the hand and he said, "Now I have you, Molly Whuppie. If I had done as much ill to you as you have done to me, what would you do to me?"

15   Molly thought fast and said, "I would put you into a sack with a cat, a dog, a needle and thread, and shears. Next, I'd hang the sack up on the wall. Then I'd get a big stick. Finally, I would take you down, still in the sack, and hit the sack."

16   "Well, Molly," said the giant, "I'll just do that to you."

17   So he put Molly in a sack with all the things she had listed. Then he hung the sack on the wall and went to get a big stick.

18   Molly, inside the sack, sang out: "Oh, if you saw what I see."

19   "Oh," said the giant's wife, "what do you see, Molly?"

20   But Molly just sang out once more, "Oh, if you saw what I see!"

21   The giant's wife begged Molly to take her up into the sack so she could see what Molly saw. So Molly took the shears and cut a hole in the sack. Then she took the needle and thread and jumped down. She then helped the giant's wife into the sack, and sewed up the hole.

22   The giant's wife saw nothing and begged to get out, but Molly simply hid herself behind a door.

23   The giant came home with a big stick and took down the sack. He raised up the stick, but did not swing it when he heard the cat mew and the dog bark. "Be quiet!" he yelled. Molly used this opportunity to sneak out. The giant saw her out of the corner of his eye and ran after her. They came to the "Bridge of One Hair." Molly got over the bridge, but the giant couldn't. The giant yelled, but Molly just ran on to the king with the ring.

24   And so Molly, the youngest and cleverest, was married to the king's youngest son, and Molly never saw the giant again.

Kate Shelley: A Young Hero

1   A fierce storm was raging on a summer evening in 1881 in Moingona, Iowa. The waters were rising in Honey Creek. Kate Shelley and her mother were looking at each other anxiously when they heard a locomotive approaching. Suddenly, there was a loud crash as the locomotive plunged off the washed-out bridge into the creek below.

2   Fifteen-year-old Kate raced outside to see if she could help. She was relieved to see that two members of the crew had escaped and were clinging to a tree above the stream. However, Kate realized that the midnight express train from Ogden was due soon. She had to do something, or it, too, was doomed.

3   She decided she would have to get to the Moingona station and tell them to hold the train from Ogden. To reach Moingona, Kate had to cross a long, high train bridge over the turbulent Des Moines River. The wind blew out her lantern and almost knocked her off the bridge, but she kept going, crawling on her hands and knees. At last she made it. Kate raced the remaining half-mile to Moingona, and told the agent about the bridge. Then she fainted.

4   The station was able to hold the train from Ogden. When Kate came to, she insisted on guiding rescuers to the men trapped at Honey Creek.

5   In recognition of Kate's heroism, the Kate Shelley High Bridge was named in her honor.

BuildReflectWrite

Build Knowledge

Identify three of Molly Whuppie's character traits. Based on those traits, describe the kind of friend you think Molly would be.

Molly Whuppie's Character Traits
1)
2)
3)
What kind of friend do you think Molly would be?

Reflect

How do we overcome obstacles?

Based on this week's texts, write down new ideas and questions you have about the essential question.

_____

_____

_____

_____

_____

Building Research Skills

Narrative

Imagine that you have been asked to write a narrative story with a giant as a villain. One of your guiding research questions is: What other fairy tales have villains who are giants? Read and take notes from two or more sources to help you answer this question. List the sources of your information.

Hercules' Quest

an excerpt from *The Three Golden Apples*

by Nathaniel Hawthorne

The myths of ancient Greece and Rome are stories of powerful gods and goddesses, courageous human heroes, and monster-like creatures. All of these characters play a part in dramatic journeys and adventures. The hero in the following passage is one of the most important figures in Greek and Roman mythology. His name is Hercules (Heracles in Greek mythology), and he is a demi-god: the son of the Roman god Jupiter (Zeus in Greek mythology) and a mortal mother. Hercules is known for his incredible strength and courage. Later, after he commits a terrible crime, he is sentenced to twelve tasks or "labors" to atone for his actions. One of these labors is to retrieve a treasure of three golden apples, guarded by nymphs called Hesperides and a many-headed giant dragon. Hercules travels a long way and goes through many trials on his quest to get the golden apples. He also gets help from Atlas, the leader of the Titans, a race of Giants.

Nathaniel Hawthorne (1804–1864) was an American novelist and short story writer. One of his most celebrated novels is The Scarlett Letter.

1   Hercules, in order to complete his quest, had to get three golden apples. He asked the giant, Atlas, about the apples and how he might get them.

2   "No one but myself can go into the garden of the Hesperides, and gather the golden apples. If it were not for this little business of holding up the sky, I would make half a dozen steps across the sea, and get them for you," said Atlas.

3   "You are very kind," replied Hercules. "Can't you rest the sky upon a mountain?"

4   "None of them are quite high enough," said Atlas, shaking his head. "You seem to be a fellow of some strength. What if you should take my burden on your shoulders, while I do your errand for you?"

5   Now Hercules was a remarkably strong man. If any mortal was capable of holding up the sky, it was Hercules. Nevertheless, it seemed so difficult an undertaking, that, for the first time in his life, he hesitated.

6   "Is the sky very heavy?" he inquired.

7   "Why, not particularly so, at first," answered the giant, shrugging his shoulders. "But it gets to be a little burdensome, after a thousand years!"

8   "And how long a time," asked the hero, "will it take you to get the golden apples?"

9   "O, that will be done in a few moments," cried Atlas. "I shall take ten or fifteen miles at a stride, and be at the garden and back again before your shoulders begin to ache."

10   "Well, then," answered Hercules, "I will climb the mountain behind you there, and relieve you of your burden."

11   So without more words, the sky was shifted from the shoulders of Atlas, and placed upon those of Hercules.

12   When this was safely accomplished, the first thing that the giant did was to stretch himself. Next, he slowly lifted one of his feet out of the forest that had grown up around it, and then, the other. Then, all at once, he began to caper, and leap, and dance, for joy at his freedom. When his joy had a little subsided, he stepped into the sea.

13   Hercules watched the giant, as he still went onward until at last the gigantic shape faded entirely out of view. And now Hercules began to consider what he should do, in case Atlas should be drowned in the sea. Or, if he were to be stung to death by the dragon with the hundred heads, which guarded the golden apples of the Hesperides. If any such misfortune were to happen, how could he ever get rid of the sky?

14   "I really pity the poor giant," thought Hercules. "If it wearies me so much in ten minutes, how must it have wearied him in a thousand years!"

15   Finally, Hercules beheld the huge shape of the giant, like a cloud, on the far-off edge of the sea. At his nearer approach, Atlas held up his hand, in which Hercules could perceive three magnificent golden apples, as big as pumpkins, all hanging from one branch.

16   "I am glad to see you again," shouted Hercules, when the giant was within hearing. "So you have got the golden apples?"

17   "Certainly, certainly," answered Atlas; "and very fair apples they are. I took the finest that grew on the tree, I assure you."

18   "I heartily thank you for your trouble. And now, as I have a long way to go, and am rather in haste—and as the king, my cousin, is anxious to receive the golden apples—will you be kind enough to take the sky off my shoulders again?" asked Hercules.

19   "Why, as to that," said the giant, chucking the golden apples into the air, twenty miles high, or thereabouts, and catching them as they came down, "as to that, my good friend, I consider you a little unreasonable. Cannot I carry the golden apples to the king, your cousin, much quicker than you could? As his majesty is in such a hurry to get them, I promise you to take my longest strides. And, besides, I have no fancy for burdening myself with the sky, just now."

20   Here Hercules grew impatient, and gave a great shrug of his shoulders. It being now twilight, you might have seen two or three stars tumble out of their places. Everybody on earth looked upward in affright, thinking that the sky might be going to fall next.

21   "O, that will never do!" cried Giant Atlas, with a great roar of laughter. "I have not let fall so many stars within the last five centuries. By the time you have stood there as long as I did, you will begin to learn patience!"

22   "What!" shouted Hercules, very wrathfully, "do you intend to make me bear this burden forever?"

23   "We will see about that, one of these days," answered the giant. "At all events, you ought not to complain, if you have to bear it the next hundred years, or perhaps the next thousand. I bore it a good while longer, in spite of the backache. Well, then, after a thousand years, if I happen to feel in the mood, we may possibly shift about again. You are certainly a very strong man, and can never have a better opportunity to prove it. Posterity will talk of you, I warrant it!"

24   "Pish!" cried Hercules, with another hitch of his shoulders. "Just take the sky upon your head one instant, will you? I want to make a cushion of my lion's skin, for the weight to rest upon. It really chafes me, and will cause unnecessary inconvenience in so many centuries as I am to stand here."

25   "That's no more than fair, and I'll do it!" replied the giant. For Atlas had no unkind feeling towards Hercules, and was merely acting with a too selfish consideration of his own ease. "For just five minutes, then, I'll take back the sky. Only for five minutes! I have no idea of spending another thousand years as I spent the last. Variety is the spice of life, say I."

26   Ah, the thick-witted old rogue of a giant! He threw down the golden apples, and received back the sky, from the head and shoulders of Hercules, upon his own, where it rightly belonged. And Hercules picked up the three golden apples. They were as big or bigger than pumpkins, and straightway set out on his journey homeward. He moved on without paying the slightest heed to the thundering tones of the giant, who bellowed after him to come back. Another forest sprang up around the giant's feet, and grew ancient there. And again might be seen oak-trees, of six or seven centuries old, that had waxed thus again betwixt his enormous toes.

27   And there stands the giant, to this day. Or, at any rate, there stands a mountain as tall as he, and which bears his name, Atlas. And when the thunder rumbles about its summit, we may imagine it to be the voice of Giant Atlas, bellowing after Hercules!

28   *Hercules completed his twelve labors successfully. He met all the challenges with courage and bravery. As a result, his honor was restored. In Roman and Greek mythology, he is the only mortal to sit with gods on Mount Olympus.*

Word Study Read

Remember
to annotate
as you read.

Notes

Paul Bunyan and the Troublesome Mosquitoes

1   Right from the start, Paul Bunyan was a giant of a human being. As a baby, he was so enormous that he had to sleep in a lumber wagon instead of a crib. Young Paul might've been dangerous, if he hadn't been kind to the core.

2   Paul grew up to become a famous lumberjack. He was so powerful that he could fell twelve trees in a single stroke. When he built his own lumber camp, it was the biggest one around.

3   Remember the summer of the troublesome mosquitoes? Well, those mosquitoes were mean, and they had a painful bite! They were so big that the lumberjacks had to fight them off with their axes.

4   However, Paul was a resourceful man. He imported some huge bees to destroy the pesky mosquitoes. Unfortunately, that just made things worse. The fearsome insects intermarried and had children that could sting like a bee and bite as often as a mosquito!

5   Their craving for sweets was their downfall. Just when the lumberjacks feared that the mosquitoes were invincible, a ship came up the river, bringing sugar to the lumber camp. The greedy insects swarmed the decks and ate so much sugar that they couldn't fly. They plummeted into the river and drowned. That evening, the grateful lumberjacks celebrated by cooking Paul's favorite dinner of flapjacks and scrambled eggs.

BuildReflectWrite

Build Knowledge

In the chart below, record your ideas about Hercules.

Hercules' Quest	
1) What are the main obstacles Hercules faces?	2) How does Hercules overcome these obstacles?
3) How would you describe Hercules?	4) In your view, is Hercules heroic?

Reflect

How do we overcome obstacles?

Based on this week's texts, write down new ideas and questions you have about the essential question.

_____

_____

_____

_____

_____

_____

Building Research Skills

Opinion

Some people think that Hercules is the greatest hero in Roman/Greek mythology. Do you agree? Imagine that you have been asked to write an opinion essay on this topic. One of your guiding research questions is: Who are other great heroes in Greek mythology? Read and take notes from two or more souces to help you answer this question. List the sources of your information.

Support for Collaborative Conversation

Discussion Prompts

Express ideas or opinions . . .

When I read _____, it made me think that _____.

Based on the information in _____, my [opinion/idea] is _____.

As I [listened to/read/watched] _____, it occurred to me that _____.

It was important that _____.

Gain the floor . . .

I would like to add a comment. _____.

Excuse me for interrupting but _____.

That made me think of _____.

Build on a peer's idea or opinion . . .

That's an interesting point. It makes me think _____.

If _____, then maybe _____.

[Name] said _____. That could mean that _____.

Express agreement with a peer's idea . . .

I agree that _____ because _____.

I also feel that _____ because _____.

[Name] made the comment that _____, and I think that is important because _____.

Respectfully express disagreement . . .

I understand your point of view that _____, but in my opinion _____ because _____.

That is an interesting idea, but did you consider the fact that _____?

I do not agree that _____. I think that _____ because _____.

Ask a clarifying question . . .

You said _____. Could you explain what you mean by that?

I don't understand how your evidence supports that inference. Can you say more?

I'm not sure I understand. Are you saying that _____?

Clarify for others . . .

When I said _____, what I meant was that _____.

I reached my conclusion because _____.

Group Roles

Discussion director:
Your role is to guide the group's discussion and be sure that everyone has a chance to express his or her ideas.

Notetaker:
Your job is to record the group's ideas and important points of discussion.

Summarizer:
In this role, you will restate the group's comments and conclusions.

Presenter:
Your role is to provide an overview of the group's discussion to the class.

Timekeeper:
You will track the time and help to keep your peers on task.

Making Meaning with Words

Word	My Definition	My Sentence
accomplished (p. 24)		
attracted (p. 6)		
burden (p. 23)		
contemptuously (p. 8)		
deceive (p. 4)		
dreadful (p. 13)		
hesitated (p. 23)		
managed (p. 14)		
perceive (p. 25)		
resolved (p. 7)		

Lexile 750L–940L

Build Knowledge Across 10 Topic Strands

 **Government and Citizenship**

Government in Action

 Character

Characters' Actions and Reactions

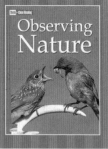 **Life Science**

Observing Nature

Point of View

Understanding Different Points of View

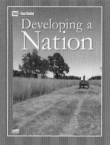 **Technology and Society**

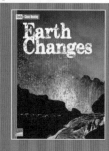

Technology for a Green Future

Theme

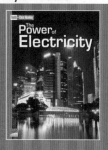

Confronting Challenges

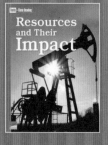 **History and Culture**

Developing a Nation

Earth Science

Earth Changes

Economics

Resources and Their Impact

Physical Science

The Power of Electricity

BENCHMARK EDUCATION COMPANY

Grade 4 • Uni

ISBN-13: 978-1-4900-

T2-EDE-361

9 781490 092027